*Ros's
love, Vernon*

SELECTED POEMS
Vernon Scannell

Allison & Busby
London

First published in 1971 by
Allison & Busby Limited, 6a Noel Street, London W.1

© 1971 Vernon Scannell

Vernon Scannell's *Selected Poems* is published
simultaneously in a paperback edition, a
hardback edition, and also in a specially
bound edition autographed by the author and
limited to fifty copies

Paperback SBN 85031 053 9
Hardback SBN 85031 054 7
Limited SBN 85031 055 5

*Printed in Great Britain by
The Bowering Press Plymouth*

Contents

From *Walking Wounded* (1965)

From *Epithets of War* (1969)

ACKNOWLEDGEMENTS are due to Eyre &
Spottiswoode for their kind permission to reprint
the poems from *Epithets of War*.

They Did Not Expect This

They did not expect this. Being neither wise nor brave
And wearing only the beauty of youth's season
They took the first turning quite unquestioningly
And walked quickly without looking back even once.

It was of course the wrong turning. First they were nagged
By a small wind that tugged at their clothing like a dog;
Then the rain began and there was no shelter anywhere,
Only the street and the rows of houses stern as soldiers.

Though the blood chilled, the endearing word burnt the
    tongue.
There were no parks or gardens or public houses:
Midnight settled and the rain paused leaving the city
Enormous and still like a great sleeping seal.

At last they found accommodation in a cold
Furnished room where they quickly learnt to believe in ghosts;
They had their hope stuffed and put on the mantelpiece
But found, after a while, that they did not notice it.

While she spends many hours looking in the bottoms of
    teacups
He reads much about association football
And waits for the marvellous envelope to fall:
Their eyes are strangers and they rarely speak. They did not
    expect this.

The Lovers Part in Winter

It seemed appropriate that it should happen
On the day when winter consolidated
Its territorial gains; when the sky's skin
Was tight with the pain of cold and all the streams
Were paralysed, still, like a photograph.

Separately they'll hate the winter from now on,
Find its beauty not their style at all,
Hating the air in which the germ of lie
Could not for an instant live. They will fear
That mass of frozen thunder, the mountain range.

The green conspirators were dead or banished,
There was no talk of bird or resurrection;
Speech lay betrayed in fragments at their feet;
The bed was cold as snow, the fire was out
And stillborn tears froze hard and cut like glass.

They had both been cruel and dishonest;
Yet pity hurt like winter when she went
Over the snow alone. And then it seemed
Her scarlet cloak, laced by the falling flakes,
Grew ermine-white except for stains of blood.

The Visitation

The fire is small and hushed, the candles' speech
Is muted to a whisper while the walls
Tremble, move closer, then nervously withdraw;
Somewhere, beyond this world, a nightbird calls.

The clock counts moments in its neat black voice,
The wind complains that night is cruel to him;
Small pools of darkness brim the shallow vales
Delved in the white plain of the counterpane.

The bed seems strangely large, the intricate
Carved posts are parodied by aggravated
Semblances that mime upon the ceiling;
Only the pillowed head is unrelated.

Only the old frail skull and waxen hands
That rest upon the counterpane seem certain,
Indifferent to the terror that informs
The room's hysteria, the frightened curtain.

The noiseless gibberish of shadows grows
More feverish; bird calls from night's dark hill
Imperious; the candles weep, the fire burns low,
The clock is ticking but the hands are still.

Gunpowder Plot

For days these curious cardboard buds have lain
In brightly coloured boxes. Soon the night
Will come. We pray there'll be no rain
To make these magic orchids flame less bright.

Now in the garden's darkness they begin
To flower: the frenzied whizz of Catherine-wheel
Puts forth its fiery petals and the thin
Rocket soars to burst upon the steel

Bulwark of a cloud. And then the guy,
Absurdly human phoenix, is again
Gulped by greedy flames: the harvest sky
Is flecked with threshed and golden grain.

'Uncle! A cannon! Watch me as I light it!'
The women, helter-skelter, squealing high,
Retreat; the paper fuse is quickly lit,
A cat-like hiss and spit of fire, a sly

Falter, then the air is shocked with blast.
The cannon bangs, and in my nostrils drifts
A bitter scent that brings the lurking past
Lurching to my side. The present shifts,

Allows a ten-year memory to walk
Unhindered now; and so I'm forced to hear
The banshee howl of mortar and the talk
Of men who died; am forced to taste my fear.

I listen for a moment to the guns,
The torn earth's grunts, recalling how I prayed.
The past retreats. I hear a corpse's sons:
'Who's scared of bangers?' 'Uncle! John's afraid!'

Old Man's Song

The baby bawling, being sick,
The spotty girl with hockey-stick
Who dreams of pink blancmange and pie,
Might not be
Ideally
Happy but I know they are
Far better off than I.

I watch the warm limbs jolly by,
Feel neither grand nor fatherly:
I don't long
For those strong
Bodies but how achingly
I desire desire.

Friday night boys as bold as Bass
Release their lusts like poison gas
In punching yells or foggy songs;
That in the end
They will descend
To my cellar does not ease
This thorny hat of wrongs.

The autumn leaves romantically
Die gay and suicidally
And night is hurt by the owl's cry;
The still sleeper
Sleeps deeper
Whom no alarming clock will shock:
He's better off than I.

Cat in the night clawing silence
Howling lust that needs no licence
Makes me want to want to die;
Even though
They don't know
Dogs and bitches bogged in ditches
Are far better off than I.

Schoolroom on a Wet Afternoon

The unrelated paragraphs of morning
Are forgotten now: the severed heads of kings
Rot by the misty Thames; the roses of York
And Lancaster are pressed between the leaves
Of history; negroes sleep in Africa.
The complexities of simple interest lurk
In inkwells and the brittle sticks of chalk:
Afternoon is come and English Grammar.

Rain falls as though the sky has been bereaved,
Stutters its inarticulate grief on glass
Of every lachrymose pane. The children read
Their books or make pretence of concentration,
Each bowed head seems bent in supplication
Or resignation to the fate that waits
In the unmapped forests of the future.
Is it their doomed innocence noon weeps for?

In each diminutive breast a human heart
Pumps out the necessary blood: desires,
Pains and ecstasies surfride each singing wave
Which breaks in darkness on the mental shores.
Each child is disciplined; absorbed and still
At his small desk. Yet lift the lid and see,
Amidst frayed books and pencils, other shapes:
Vicious rope, glaring blade, the gun cocked to kill.

The Word of Love

Perhaps it found its perfect expression
Early in life, in the fairy-tale time,
Concerning itself with a character out of fiction,
The sleeping princess or glittering snow queen,
Or focused mutely and profoundly on
A furry bear whose solitary eye was a sad button.

Certainly, as I grew tall and gruff
And the blood of the bear turned into straw
I somehow lost the habit of love.
The leggy girls, whose sharp heels tore
My flimsy dreams, with laughter crushed
The flower at the heart of my lunar lust.

Uncertain now, myopic with peering
At celluloid legends and paper lies,
The one word breaks on my disbelieving;
And yet, and yet, the dumb heart bears
The syllable like a child in its stillness
And your present absence is a mortal illness.

The Lynching

They rode back in trap or Ford or Cadillac.
Behind them on the tree upon the hill
Beneath the non-committal dark
Star-punctured sky their deed hung still
And black. They rode fast. One might have thought
That they were being pursued; their speed
Lunged forward with a long arm through the night
To drag the small town to their need.
And in the town the white wives in their white
Nightgowns listened to the clock
And with their wide-eyed fingers plucked
Those gowns which, fastened at the neck
And neat at feet, need not be roughed that night
To prove their husbands' manhood, or the lack.

Remembrance Day

Apposite blood red the blobs
Of artificial poppies count
Our annual dead.
The garment of lament is worn
Threadbare and each medal hangs
Heavy its shameful head.

Bugles make their sad assault
Upon the heart and spine and throat
Ordering regret.
The names evoked are usual:
Passchendaele, Bapaume and Loos—
Our cheeks are wet.

And fumbling for the right response
We summon names more personal:
Nobby, Frank and Ted.
But wormy years have eaten their
Identities and none can mourn
These artificial dead.

And when a true emotion strikes
It strikes a crude, unsanctioned blow
Which brings a harsher chill
To hearts that know that they grow old
And must grow older yet before
That terrible Until.

Formal Problem

The poet, in his garden, holds his pen
Like a dart between two fingers and a thumb;
The target is unfortunately blurred;
He does not see as clearly as when young,
Or, rather, doubt and nervousness obtrude:
He dare not risk the unreflecting fling.

How to convey the taste and texture of
This sun-drunk afternoon? How can he sieve
The essence of these greens, the grass, the trees,
The mating scents, the way the clouds behave,
And shape it to a pattern which might please
The glinting intellect and hungry Five?

And how include the aeroplane which slides
No larger than a pearl across the skies,
Its roar wrapped up in distance which conceals
A figure masked and helmeted whose strong
Finger stabs the button that resolves
The poet's problem in a flash, and bang.

Killing Flies

Compelled by their black hum
And accidental mischief, I,
Distracted from my pompous play
With words that twist and tease,
Rolled myself a paper club
And stalked my quick tormentors round
The room until they settled on
The wall, their mortuary slab.
Three I translated with one swipe
From busy bodies into dark
Smudges on my wall
Before I knew my action wrong
And guiltily let fall
The paper truncheon and went back
To where my words like insects bled
And dried upon their paper shroud,
All dead, unquestionably dead.

Two Appearances

The lean ecstatic man, the starry poet,
Expecting any day the total vision
And generously preparing to bestow it
On all of us, despite some mild derision
From that minority who doubtless find
His meditative beauty not their kind,
Walks whitely like a batsman to his crease;
While in the dirty night the ugly fellow,
His barrel belly resting on his thighs,
Calls out the temptress with a soundless bellow
And fixes her with angry bloodshot eyes,
Then forces her to bear a masterpiece.

Simon Frailman:
TEN SONNETS AND AN ELEGIAC CODA

First Sight

Simon Frailman, six feet in his dreams,
A thickening five feet eight when morning rings
And pricks him with insistent questionings:
Why did he never wear those uniforms,
The plumage and caparisons, bear arms
Or, over one heroic nipple, wings?
And now it is too late. The evening brings
A smoky sadness to the mortgaged lawns.

A moderate man with no intemperate lusts,
Content to tame the rose and civilise
The lawless strawberry, he guards the trust
Of wife and children and will never slip
The marriage leash; his quaint adulteries
Performed with lawful spouse at his thick hip.

Simon on Sunday

Printed rumours rustle through the morning.
The fragrant chamber music of the bacon
Is drowned by richer chords of roast and pudding
As Simon sprays and weeds his timid garden.
The spectres of the earlier bells compel
A melancholy that is hard to pardon
While birds in shimmering trees are simmering still
And thin stems bend beneath their fragile burden.

Evening is listless, fat with Monday morning;
Time tells its dirty secret to the heart;

The fiddles and the saxophones are moaning
As venal meat is prinked with spurious art.
A sudden chill knifes Simon to the bone:
He sees a waiting Sunday, barren as a stone.

Simon Drunk ...

'It's not too late,' the glass says to his lips;
'It's not too late,' the whisper in the bowel.
The glasses wink and chink, the cigarettes
Are wagging words, but Simon draws apart.
He will be Gauguin, paint outrageous tarts,
Learn Greek, read Proust and do P.T. each day;
Write a witty novel or a play
And lead the leading lady well astray.

'It's not too late,' his lips say to his glass.
He feels the fireworks flowering in the dark
Beneath his sober shirt. He'll tell his boss
Just what he thinks of him and find some work
In Paris, Athens, Rome. ... Then Mrs. Frailman spoke:
'The Party's over, Simon. Let's go home.'

... And Simon Sober

An ashen dawn begins in Simon's mouth.
The conscious day unglues his sleep to drop
Some broken recollections in his lap
And snigger with unsympathetic mirth.
He sees himself, absurd, immodest, vain,
Swaying from maudlin right to left of wrath,
Exciting pursed contempt or nervous ruth,
His dignity, like trousers, fallen down.

The day, a soft groan, greys towards its end
Sustained by aspirin and Worcester Sauce;
A misty sexuality, a wind
Of speechless longing drifts towards his sleep
Where he, marooned upon a small remorse,
Builds resolutions he will never keep.

The Good Temptation

Frailman alone, peaceful in the sweet
Tobacco educating simple air,
Feels a spectral elbow nudge the heart
And knows what Newman knew when tempted by
Not venery but virtue, holy snare
Which draws the chosen victim to the high
Pinnacle which looks upon the wheat
Immortal and the golden everywhere.

Yet how resistible temptation of this sort.
Soon spirit aches and squints at such a glare,
And Simon turns away upon the thought
Of leaving his terrain to sojourn there
Where he may never see, or need to see,
The white and delicate legs more winkingly.

Simon Perplexed

Then Simon thinks how difficult to feel
Real love when there is no reflected pleasure,
And knows he never could sincerely kneel
To intercede for one who had his measure.

He might whip up a plausible compassion
For those whose sins are operatic, loud,

Or those whose moral dress is out of fashion,
Whose bloody heads are tinted but unbowed.

But not a simulacrum of affection
Can he display for virtue's household guard
Whose faces, even after resurrection,
Would still resemble watchful bags of lard.

And Simon swears if these are such as dwell
In Paradise, then heaven must be pure hell.

Father

Owl tinctured, blind, the wind sighs through the night,
Then mimics, with a sudden lift, a cry
Of infant fear, and Simon sits upright,
Pricked quick by this pathetic fallacy.
But none, alas, of Frailman's children now
Perturbs the evening with needs sad or shrill:
Two crude and violent boys, both low of brow,
A ten-year girl of double-barrelled will.

They do not need him now to heave them out
Of wells of furry fear or scare away
With one electric slap the grunting snout
That sniffed their beds: yet if they should display
A leaf of love his pleasure is immense
And humble from the heart's intelligence.

Simon Sans Teeth

This is a stage from which there's no retreat,
Thinks Simon sadly; the lost familiars leave
A sibilance that hisses of senility;

His smile is false indeed. He cannot eat.
And Mrs. Frailman and his friends deceive
Themselves, not him, when they repeatedly
Assure him that, before much longer, he
Will treat them as his own, contemptuously.

But though, for work, these teeth prove adequate
He knows and always will that they are false.
A part of him has died and, soon or late,
The rest of him must follow till that hour
When he can buy no artificial pulse
And his dead grin will gleam in some dark drawer.

Birthday Present

Forty-six years since Simon bawled his first
And unavailing no at being forced
To put on short mortality and thrust
His midget head through life's enormous noose
Which now, perceptibly, is much less loose.

He once believed his rampant greed and lust
Would leave their ageing cage or that, at least,
They'd drowse replete, resavouring the past;
And he would hang his fears and vanity
Upon a hook in dim serenity.

But through the jungle of his nerves the lithe
And tigerish beauties creep; now he could swear,
Until the rope of years pulls tight, he'll writhe
And hear the wanton whisperings everywhere.

Simon Gay

No causing in the sky or envelope
But joy, like oxygen, is everywhere;
And though he knows a hostile periscope
May surface soon and fix him with its glare
He rides the sparkling crest and flies his smile,
Gay in the face of preying buccaneers;
And though the clouds may shortly belch with bile
He will not shut his eyes or plug his ears.

These spells are brief and magical. He knows
Before the day is out he'll run aground
Or be capsized by envious torpedoes
Then cast up on some chill barbaric isle:
Yet Simon vows, though grievous reefs abound,
Whatever comes, the voyage is well worth while.

Elegiac Coda

And when the wingèd chariot at last
Accelerates and runs him down, what then?
No melancholy flags will sag half-mast,
The pubs will close at the usual half-past ten;
The lions in the square will be dry eyed;
No newspaper will note that he has died.

But Frailman's children, burly now or tall,
Will find with slight astonishment that he
Bequeaths, with lesser valuables, a small
And wholly disconcerting legacy:
A foliate grief that opens like a fist
To show a love they doubted could exist.

And Mrs. Frailman, staring at a chair,
Whose occupant contrives by not being there
To occupy it far more poignantly
Than when his flesh flopped in it wearily,
Will know that he has cleared a way which she
Must follow after, that more easily.

The Jealous Wife

Like a private eye she searches
For clues through diaries and papers;
Examines his clothing for the guilty stains
Of crimson lipstick, wicked wine,
Or something biological.
And when no act of sensual
Crime can be at length surmised
She is most puzzled and surprised
To be assailed by disappointment
Not relief. Her steel intent
Is never to betray to him
The blonde and naked thoughts within
The purple bedroom of her mind,
But her resolve can never stand
The pressure of the need to know:
'Where?' she says and 'When?' and 'Who?'
'What time?' 'What day?' The question-marks
Like powerful iron grappling hooks
Drag him to her fantasy.
And then he cannot fail to see
Within the harem of her skull
The lovely wickednesses loll.
Thus, at night, they softly creep,
Tap at the darkened panes of sleep;
Then, white and tender, glide inside
His dream on whose delightful slope
At last her fears are justified.

Silver Wedding

The party is over and I sit among
The flotsam that its passing leaves,
The dirty glasses and fag-ends:
Outside, a black wind grieves.

Two decades and a half of marriage;
It does not really seem as long,
And yet I find I have scant knowledge
Of youth's ebullient song.

David, my son, my loved rival,
And Julia, my tapering daughter,
Now grant me one achievement only:
I turn their wine to water.

And Helen, partner of all these years,
Helen my spouse, my sack of sighs,
Reproaches me for every hurt
With injured bovine eyes.

There must have been passion once, I grant,
But neither she nor I could bear
To have its ghost come prowling from
Its dark and frowsy lair.

And we, to keep our nuptials warm,
Still wage sporadic, fireside war;
Numb with insult each yet strives
To scratch the other raw.

Twenty-five years we've now survived;
I'm not sure either why or how
As I sit with a wreath of quarrels set
On my tired and balding brow.

The Masks of Love

We did not understand that it was there,
The love we hungered for; it even seemed
Love's enemies, indifference, distaste
And cruelty, informed our father's stare
Of pained reproof, the homiletic tongue,
The sudden rage, and mother's graven face;
But we were wrong.
And when the chalk-faced master showed his teeth
And pickled us in hurtful verbiage
We labelled him Misanthropos and swore
That his vocation was revenge. But this
Was not the truth.
And later, when the easy woman gave
Free scholarship to study at the warm
College of her flesh, we called her coarse,
Promiscuous, and cunning to behave
With subsequent incontinent remorse.
We thought that we were lucky to evade
Her plot to eat us up alive, but we
Were just about as wrong as we could be.
As afterwards we were, when our sweet dove
That we had welcomed to the marriage cote
Became a beaky squawker and appeared
To loathe the bargain that her instincts bought:
And we did not permit her to reveal
The tender fingers in the iron glove
Like that whose knuckled stratagems conceal
A desperate and brooding love.

Poem for Jane

So many catalogues have been
Compiled by poets, good and bad,
Of qualities that they would wish
To see their infant daughters wear;
Or lacking children they have clad
Others' daughters in the bright
Imagined garments of the flesh,
Prayed for jet or golden hair
Or for the inconspicuous
Homespun of the character
That no one ever whistles after.
Dear Jane, whatever I may say
I'm sure approving whistles will
Send you like an admiral on
Ships of welcome in a bay
Of tender waters where the fish
Will surface longing to be meshed
Among the treasure of your hair.
And as for other qualities
There's only one I really wish
To see you amply manifest
And that's a deep capacity
For loving; and I long for this
Not for any lucky one
Who chances under your love's sun
But because, without it, you
Would never know completely joy
As I know joy through loving you.

Jane at Play

I watch her in the garden and enjoy
Her serious enjoyment as she bends
And murmurs her grave nonsense to the toy
Circle of her animals and friends;
The doll that she quite obviously likes best
Would be to other eyes the ugliest.

For it is only later that we choose
To favour things which publish our good taste,
Whose beauty proves our talent to refuse
To dote upon the comic or defaced;
Unlike the child who needs no reference
Or cautious map to find her preference.

Yet we may be deceived by some old trick,
Robbed of our bright expensive instruments
And bundled from our path into the thick
Frondescence strangling all our arguments,
As when we see our child's plain loveliness
And blunder blind into our happiness.

The Terrible Abstractions

The naked hunter's fist, bunched round his spear,
Was tight and wet inside with sweat of fear;
He heard behind him what the hunted hear.

The silence in the undergrowth crept near;
Its mischief tickled in his nervous ear
And he became the prey, the quivering deer.

The naked hunter feared the threat he knew:
Being hunted, caught, then slaughtered like a ewe
By beasts who padded on four legs or two.

The naked hunter in the bus or queue
Under his decent wool is frightened too
But not of what his hairy forebear knew.

The terrible abstractions prowl about
The compound of his fear and chronic doubt;
He keeps fires burning boldly all night through,
But cannot keep the murderous shadows out.

Incendiary

That one small boy with a face like pallid cheese
And burnt-out little eyes could make a blaze
As brazen, fierce and huge, as red and gold
And zany yellow as the one that spoiled
Three thousand guineas' worth of property
And crops at Godwin's Farm on Saturday
Is frightening—as fact and metaphor:
An ordinary match intended for
The lighting of a pipe or kitchen fire
Misused may set a whole menagerie
Of flame-fanged tigers roaring hungrily.
And frightening, too, that one small boy should set
The sky on fire and choke the stars to heat
Such skinny limbs and such a little heart
Which would have been content with one warm kiss
Had there been anyone to offer this.

A Sense of Danger

The city welcomed us. Its favoured sons,
Holders of office, prosperous and plump
With meat and honours, said, 'Put down your guns,
There's nothing here to fear. The industrial slump,
The Plague, the hunting-packs, the underfed,
All are gone, all caged or safely dead.

'Rest easy here. Put down your loads and stay,
And we will purify you with the kiss
Of sweet hygienic needles and display
Incredible varieties of bliss;
We'll strip your inhibitions off like trousers.
Relax. Don't brood. You'll be as safe as houses.'

But we declined, took up our guns and bags;
Turning blind backs on offers of delight
Left for the gaunt terrain and squinting crags;
With luck we'd find a water hole that night.
'As safe as houses,' they had called the town;
But we had seen great houses tumbled down.

Ageing Schoolmaster

And now another autumn morning finds me
  With chalk dust on my sleeve and in my breath,
Preoccupied with vague, habitual speculation
  On the huge inevitability of death.

Not wholly wretched, yet knowing absolutely
  That I shall never reacquaint myself with joy,
I sniff the smell of ink and chalk and my mortality
  And think of when I rolled, a gormless boy,

And rollicked round the playground of my hours,
  And wonder when precisely tolled the bell
Which summoned me from summer liberties
  And brought me to this chill autumnal cell

From which I gaze upon the april faces
  That gleam before me, like apples ranged on shelves,
And yet I feel no pinch or prick of envy
  Nor would I have them know their sentenced selves.

With careful effort I can separate the faces,
  The dull, the clever, the various shapes and sizes,
But in the autumn shades I find I only
  Brood upon death, who carries off all the prizes.

The Telephone Number

Searching for a lost address I find,
Among dead papers in a dusty drawer,
A diary which has lain there quite ten years,
And soon forget what I am looking for,
Intrigued by cryptic entries in a hand
Resembling mine but noticeably more
Vigorous than my present quavering scrawl.
Appointments—kept or not, I don't remember—
With people now grown narrow, fat or bald;
A list of books that somehow I have never
Found the time to read, nor ever shall,
Remind me that my world is growing cold.
And then I find a scribbled code and number,
The urgent words: 'Must not forget to call.'
But now, of course, I have no recollection
Of telephoning anyone at all.
The questions whisper: Did I dial that number
And, if I did, what kind of voice replied?
Questions that will never find an answer
Unless—the thought is serpentine—I tried
To telephone again, as years ago
I did, or meant to do. What would I find
If now I lifted this mechanic slave
Black to my ear and spun the dial—so . . . ?
Inhuman, impolite, the double burp
Erupts, insulting hope. The long dark sleeve
Of silence stretches out. No stranger's voice
Slips in, suspicious, cold; no manic speech
Telling what I do not wish to know

Nor throaty message creamed with sensual greed—
Nothing of these. And, when again I try,
Relief is tearful when there's no reply.

Felo de Se

Alone, he came to his decision,
The sore tears stiffening his cheeks
As headlamps flicked the ceiling with white dusters
And darkness roared downhill with nervous brakes.
Below, the murmuring and laughter,
The baritone, tobacco-smelling jokes;
And then his misery and anger
Suddenly became articulate:
'I wish that I was dead. Oh, they'll be sorry then.
I hate them and I'll kill myself tomorrow.
I want to die. I hate them, hate them. Hate.'

And kill himself in fact he did,
But not next day as he'd decided.
The deed itself, for thirty years deferred,
Occurred one wintry night when he was loaded.
Belching with scotch and misery
He turned the gas tap on and placed his head
Gently, like a pudding, in the oven.
'I want to die. I'll hurt them yet,' he said.
And once again: 'I hate them, hate them. Hate.'
The lampless darkness roared inside his head,
Then sighed into a silence in which played
The grown-up voices, still up late,
Indifferent to his rage as to his fate.

The Fair

Music and yellow steam, the fizz
Of spinning lights as roundabouts
Galloping nowhere whirl and whizz
Through fusillades of squeals and shouts;
The night sniffs rich at pungent spice,
Brandysnap and diesel oil;
The stars like scattered beads of rice
Sparsely fleck the sky's deep soil
Dulled and diminished by these trapped
Melodic meteors below
In whose feigned fever brightly lapped
The innocent excitements flow.
Pocketfuls of simple thrills
Jingle silver, purchasing
A warm and sugared fear that spills
From dizzy car and breathless swing.

So no one hears the honest shriek
From the field beyond the fair,
A single voice becoming weak,
Then dying on the ignorant air.
And not for hours will frightened love
Rise and seek her everywhere,
Then find her, like a fallen glove,
Soiled and crumpled, lying there.

Dead Dog

One day I found a lost dog in the street.
The hairs about its grin were spiked with blood,
And it lay still as stone. It must have been
A little dog, for though I only stood
Nine inches for each one of my four years
I picked it up and took it home. My mother
Squealed, and later father spaded out
A bed and tucked my mongrel down in mud.

I can't remember any feeling but
A moderate pity, cool not swollen-eyed;
Almost a godlike feeling now it seems.
My lump of dog was ordinary as bread.
I have no recollection of the school
Where I was taught my terror of the dead.

Autobiographical Note

Beeston, the place, near Nottingham:
We lived there for three years or so.
Each Saturday at two-o'clock
We queued up for the matinée,
All the kids for streets around
With snotty noses, giant caps,
Cut down coats and heavy boots,
The natural enemies of cops
And schoolteachers. Profane and hoarse
We scrambled, yelled and fought until
The Picture Palace opened up
And we, like Hamelin children, forced
Our bony way into the hall.
That much is easy to recall;
Also the reek of chewing-gum,
Gob-stoppers and liquorice,
But of the flickering myths themselves
Not much remains. The hero was
A milky wide-brimmed hat, a shape
Astride the arched white stallion;
The villain's horse and hat were black.
Disbelief did not exist
And laundered virtue always won
With quicker gun and harder fist,
And all of us applauded it.
Yet I remember moments when
In solitude I'd find myself
Brooding on the sooty man,
The bristling villain, who could move
Imagination in a way
The well-shaved hero never could,

And even warm the nervous heart
With something oddly close to love.

The Great War

Whenever war is spoken of
I find
The war that was called Great invades the mind:
The grey militia marches over land
A darker mood of grey
Where fractured tree-trunks stand
And shells, exploding, open sudden fans
Of smoke and earth.
Blind murders scythe
The deathscape where the iron brambles writhe;
The sky at night
Is honoured with rosettes of fire,
Flares that define the corpses on the wire
As terror ticks on wrists at zero hour.
These things I see,
But they are only part
Of what it is that slyly probes the heart:
Less vivid images and words excite
The sensuous memory
And, even as I write,
Fear and a kind of love collaborate
To call each simple conscript up
For quick inspection:
Trenches' parapets
Paunchy with sandbags; bandoliers, tin-hats,
Candles in dug-outs,
Duckboards, mud and rats.
Then, like patrols, tunes creep into the mind:
A long, long trail, The Rose of No-Man's Land,
Home Fires and *Tipperary*;
And through the misty keening of a band

Of Scottish pipes the proper names are heard
Like fateful commentary of distant guns:
Passchendaele, Bapaume, and Loos, and Mons.
And now,
Whenever the November sky
Quivers with a bugle's hoarse, sweet cry,
The reason darkens; in its evening gleam
Crosses and flares, tormented wire, grey earth
Splattered with crimson flowers,
And I remember,
Not the war I fought in
But the one called Great
Which ended in a sepia November
Four years before my birth.

Cows in Red Pasture

Last summer in a Kentish field
I saw the plush green darkened by
A whim of light and darkened too
By whiteness of the sheep which stood
Diminished by the distance so
They looked like gravestones on the green,
So still and small and white they seemed.
As this warm memory blurs and fades,
The emptiness bequeathed instructs
Me, curiously, to resurrect
An older memory of a field
Which I would rather far forget:
A foreign field, a field of France,
In which there lay two cows, one white
With maps of black stamped on its hide,
The other just the colour of
The caramel that I once loved.
Both were still; the toffee one
Lay on its back, its stiff legs stuck
Up from the swollen belly like
A huge discarded set of bagpipes.
The piebald cow lay on its side
Looking like any summer beast
Until one saw it had no head.

The grass on which they lay was red.

My Father's Face

Each morning, when I shave, I see his face,
Or something like a sketch of it gone wrong;
The artist caught, it seems, more than a trace
Of that uneasy boldness and the strong
Fear behind the stare which tried to shout
How tough its owner was, inviting doubt.

And though this face is altogether more
Loosely put together, and indeed
A lot less handsome, weaker in the jaw
And softer in the mouth, I feel no need
To have it reassembled, made a better
Copy of the face of its begetter.

I do not mind because my mouth is not
That lipless hyphen, military, stern;
He had the face that faces blade and shot
In schoolboys' tales, and even schoolboys learn
To laugh at it. But they've not heard it speak
Those bayonet words that guard the cruel and weak.

For weakness was his one consistency;
And when I scrape the soapy fluff away
I see that he bequeathed this gift to me
Along with various debts I cannot pay.
But he gave, too, this mirror-misting breath
Whose mercy dims the looking-glass of death;

For which kind accident I thank him now
And, though I cannot love him, feel a sort
Of salty tenderness, remembering how

The prude and lecher in him moiled and fought
Their roughhouse in the dark ring of his pride
And killed each other when his body died.

This morning, as I shave, I find I can
Forgive the blows, the meanness and the lust,
The ricochetting arsenal of a man
Who groaned groin-deep in hope's ironic dust;
But these eyes in the glass regard the living
Features with distaste, quite unforgiving.

An Old Lament Renewed

The soil is savoury with their bones' lost marrow;
    Down among dark roots their polished knuckles lie,
And no one could tell one peeled head from another;
    Earth packs each crater that once gleamed with eye.

Colonel and batman, emperor and assassin,
    Democratized by silence and corruption,
Defy identification with identical grin:
    The joke is long, will brook no interruption.

At night the imagination walks like a ghoul
    Among the stone lozenges and counterpanes of turf
Tumescent under cypresses; the long, rueful call
    Of the owl soars high and then wheels back to earth.

And brooding over the enormous dormitory
    The mind grows shrill at those nothings in lead rooms
Who were beautiful once or dull and ordinary,
    But loved, all loved, all called to sheltering arms.

Many I grieve with a grave, deep love
    Who are deep in the grave, whose faces I never saw:
Poets who died of alcohol, bullets, or birthdays
    Doss in the damp house, forbidden now to snore.

And in a French orchard lies whatever is left
    Of my friend, Gordon Rennie, whose courage would
        toughen
The muscle of resolution; he laughed
    At death's serious face, but once too often.

On summer evenings when the religious sun stains
   The gloom in the bar and the glasses surrender demurely
I think of Donovan whose surrender was unconditional,
   That great thirst swallowed entirely.

And often some small thing will summon the memory
   Of my small son, Benjamin. A smile is his sweet ghost.
But behind, in the dark, the white twigs of his bones
   Form a pattern of guilt and waste.

I am in mourning for the dull, the heroic and the mad;
   In the haunted nursery the child lies dead.
I mourn the hangman and his bulging complement;
   I mourn the cadaver in the egg.

The one-eyed rider aims, shoots death into the womb;
   Blood on the sheet of snow, the maiden dead.
The dagger has a double blade and meaning,
   So has the double bed.

Imagination swaggers in the sensual sun
   But night will find it at the usual mossy gate;
The whisper from the mouldering darkness comes:
   'I am the one you love and fear and hate.'

I know my grieving is made thick by terror;
   The bones of those I loved aren't fleshed by sorrow.
I mourn the deaths I've died and go on dying;
   I fear the long, implacable tomorrow.

Autumn

It is the football season once more
And the back pages of the Sunday papers
Again show the blurred anguish of goalkeepers.

In Maida Vale, Golders Green and Hampstead
Lamps ripen early in the surprising dusk;
They are furred like stale rinds with a fuzz of mist.

The pavements of Kensington are greasy;
The wind smells of burnt porridge in Bayswater,
And the leaves are mushed to silence in the gutter.

The big hotel like an anchored liner
Rides near the park; lit windows hammer the sky.
Like the slow swish of surf the tyres of taxis sigh.

On Ealing Broadway the cinema glows
Warm behind glass while mellow the church clock
    chimes
As the waiting girls stir in their delicate chains.

Their eyes are polished by the wind,
But the gleam is dumb, empty of joy or anger.
Though the lovers are long in coming the girls still
    linger.

We are nearing the end of the year.
Under the sombre sleeve the blood ticks faster
And in the dark ear of Autumn quick voices whisper.

It is a time of year that's to my taste,
Full of spiced rumours, sharp and velutinous flavours,
Dim with the mist that softens the cruel surfaces,
Makes mirrors vague. It is the mist that I most favour.

Talking of Death

My friend was dead. A simple sentence ended
With one black stop, like this: My friend was dead.
I had no notion that I had depended
So much on fires he lit, on that good bread
He always had to offer if I came
Hungry and cold to his inviting room.
Absurdly, I believed that he was lame
Until I started limping from his tomb.
My sorrow was the swollen, prickly kind,
Not handsome mourning smartly cut and pressed:
An actual grief, I swear. Therefore to find
Myself engaged upon a shameful quest
For anyone who'd known him, but who thought
That he was still alive, was something strange,
Something disquieting; for what I sought
Was power and presence beyond my usual range.
For once, my audience listened, welcomed me,
Avid for every syllable that spoke
Of woven fear and grieving. Nervously
They eyed my black, ambassadorial cloak.
Their faces greyed; my friend's death died, and they
Saw theirs walk in alive. I felt quite well—
Being Death's man—until they went away,
And I was left with no one else to tell.

Act of Love

This is not the man that women choose,
This honest fellow, stuffed to the lips with groans,
Whose passion cannot even speak plain prose
But grunts and mumbles in the muddiest tones.
His antics are disgusting or absurd,
His lust obtrusive, craning from its nest
At awkward times its blind reptilian head;
His jealousy and candour are a pest.

Now here is the boy that women will lie down for,
The snappy actor, skilled in the lover's part,
A lyric fibber and subvocal tenor
Whose pleasure in the play conceals his art;
Who, even as he enters her warm yes,
Hears fluttering hands and programmes in the vast
Auditorium beyond her voice
Applauding just one member of the cast.

Telephoning Her

The dial spins back, clicks still. Just half an inch
Of silence, then the abrupt eruption blurts
Its two quick jets of noise into his ear.
Again the double spurt; again. Three, four.
She does not answer. Give her just two more.
Yet still he holds the instrument to his ear,
But no longer is imagination bare.
Inside his head the room assumes its shape:
The dishevelled bed, a stocking on the floor.
The tortured clown grimaces in his frame;
The room seems empty, but how can he be sure?
And with uncertainty the light grows dim,
But not before he sees a movement there,
Quick twitching of the coverings on the bed,
Or thinks he might have noticed something stir.
Darkness grows thick as tar. Then he can hear—
Though not in the liquorice-black thing that he holds—
Her voice, thick with the body's joy and mind's despair,
Moaning a foreign word, a stranger's name.
Derisively the darkness jerks again,
Spits twice into his violated ear.

Voyeur

Find the hidden face. A prize is offered.
The scene is green and summer. On the grass
The dresses spread, exhausted butterflies,
And smooth brown legs make soft confessions to
Rough trousers. Excited air
Is hushed with kissing.
Now search for the solitary, the uncoupled one:
Not in the leafy tentacles of trees,
He is no climber,
But close to earth, well-hidden, squat.
You see him now? Yes, there! His snarling grin
Bearded with leaves, his body bushed,
Invisible. See how his eyes are fat with glee
And horror. They fizz with unfulfilment's booze.
His tongue makes sure his lips are still in place
With quick red pats.
You've found him now, and you can take your prize,
Though, as you see, we do not offer cash:
Just recognition and its loaded cosh.

Walking Wounded

A mammoth morning moved grey flanks and groaned.
In the rusty hedges pale rags of mist hung;
The gruel of mud and leaves in the mauled lane
Smelled sweet, like blood. Birds had died or flown,
Their green and silent attics sprouting now
With branches of leafed steel, hiding round eyes
And ripe grenades ready to drop and burst.
In the ditch at the cross-roads the fallen rider lay
Hugging his dead machine and did not stir
At crunch of mortar, tantrum of a Bren
Answering a Spandau's manic jabber.
Then into sight the ambulances came,
Stumbling and churning past the broken farm,
The amputated sign-post and smashed trees,
Slow wagonloads of bandaged cries, square trucks
That rolled on ominous wheels, vehicles
Made mythopoeic by their mortal freight
And crimson crosses on the dirty white.
This grave procession passed, though, for a while,
The grinding of their engines could be heard,
A dark noise on the pallor of the morning,
Dark as dried blood; and then it faded, died.
The road was empty, but it seemed to wait—
Like a stage which knows the cast is in the wings—
Wait for a different traffic to appear.
The mist still hung in snags from dripping thorns;
Absent-minded guns still sighed and thumped.
And then they came, the walking wounded,
Straggling the road like convicts loosely chained,
Dragging at ankles exhaustion and despair.
Their heads were weighted down by last night's lead,

And eyes still drank the dark. They trailed the night
Along the morning road. Some limped on sticks;
Others wore rough dressings, splints and slings;
A few had turbanned heads, the dirty cloth
Brown-badged with blood. A humble brotherhood,
Not one was suffering from a lethal hurt,
They were not magnified by noble wounds,
There was no splendour in that company.
And yet, remembering after eighteen years,
In the heart's throat a sour sadness stirs;
Imagination pauses and returns
To see them walking still, but multiplied
In thousands now. And when heroic corpses
Turn slowly in their decorated sleep
And every ambulance has disappeared
The walking wounded still trudge down that lane,
And when recalled they must bear arms again.

A Case of Murder

They should not have left him there alone,
Alone that is except for the cat.
He was only nine, not old enough
To be left alone in a basement flat,
Alone, that is, except for the cat.
A dog would have been a different thing,
A big gruff dog with slashing jaws,
But a cat with round eyes mad as gold,
Plump as a cushion with tucked-in paws—
Better have left him with a fair-sized rat!
But what they did was leave him with a cat.
He hated that cat; he watched it sit,
A buzzing machine of soft black stuff,
He sat and watched and he hated it,
Snug in its fur, hot blood in a muff,
And its mad gold stare and the way it sat
Crooning dark warmth: he loathed all that.
So he took Daddy's stick and he hit the cat.
Then quick as a sudden crack in glass
It hissed, black flash, to a hiding place
In the dust and dark beneath the couch,
And he followed the grin on his new-made face,
A wide-eyed, frightened snarl of a grin,
And he took the stick and he thrust it in,
Hard and quick in the furry dark.
The black fur squealed and he felt his skin
Prickle with sparks of dry delight.
Then the cat again came into sight,
Shot for the door that wasn't quite shut,
But the boy, quick too, slammed fast the door:
The cat, half-through, was cracked like a nut

And the soft black thud was dumped on the floor.
Then the boy was suddenly terrified
And he bit his knuckles and cried and cried;
But he had to do something with the dead thing there.
His eyes squeezed beads of salty prayer
But the wound of fear gaped wide and raw;
He dared not touch the thing with his hands
So he fetched a spade and shovelled it
And dumped the load of heavy fur
In the spidery cupboard under the stair
Where it's been for years, and though it died
It's grown in that cupboard and its hot low purr
Grows slowly louder year by year:
There'll not be a corner for the boy to hide
When the cupboard swells and all sides split
And the huge black cat pads out of it.

Hide and Seek

Call out. Call loud: 'I'm ready! Come and find me!'
The sacks in the toolshed smell like the seaside.
They'll never find you in this salty dark,
But be careful that your feet aren't sticking out.
Wiser not to risk another shout.
The floor is cold. They'll probably be searching
The bushes near the swing. Whatever happens
You mustn't sneeze when they come prowling in.
And here they are, whispering at the door;
You've never heard them sound so hushed before.
Don't breathe. Don't move. Stay dumb. Hide in your
    blindness.
They're moving closer, someone stumbles, mutters;
Their words and laughter scuffle, and they're gone.
But don't come out just yet; they'll try the lane
And then the greenhouse and back here again.
They must be thinking that you're very clever,
Getting more puzzled as they search all over.
It seems a long time since they went away.
Your legs are stiff, the cold bites through your coat;
The dark damp smell of sand moves in your throat.
It's time to let them know that you're the winner.
Push off the sacks. Uncurl and stretch. That's better!
Out of the shed and call to them: 'I've won!
Here I am! Come and own up I've caught you!'
The darkening garden watches. Nothing stirs.
The bushes hold their breath; the sun is gone.
Yes, here you are. But where are they who sought you?

Six Year Darling

The poets are to blame, or partly so:
Wordsworth's pretty pigmy, plump with joy,
And Henry Vaughan's white celestial thoughts
Mislead as much as Millais' chubby boy
Or daddy-blessing Christopher at prayer.
These fantasies are still quite popular.
Pick up any children's book and you will see
That all the illustrations are as false
As muscle-builders' ads: angelic girls
And sturdy little chaps with candid eyes—
Not to please the children, understand;
You'll find few kids who're kidded by the act,
Though later most of them will take the bribe
And speak of infancy as paradise.
Will this boy, here, be legatee of lies?
Perhaps he will, and maybe just as well
If one day he is going to breed his own.
But now he knows that things are otherwise:
Not paradise, no glimpse of God's bright face,
But time of simple goods like warmth and sweets,
Excitement, too; but often pain and fear,
And worse than either, boredom, long and grey,
A dusty road to nowhere, hard to walk,
Going on and on, desolate and bare,
Until it breaks upon the hidden dark.

I'm Covered Now

'What would happen to your lady wife
And little ones—you've four I think you said—
Little ones I mean, not wives, ha-ha—
What would happen to them if . . .' And here
He cleared his throat of any reticence.
'. . . if something happened to you? We've got to face
These things, must be realistic, don't you think?
Now, we have various schemes to give you cover
And, taking in account your age and means,
This policy would seem to be the one . . '

The words uncoiled, effortless but urgent,
Assured, yet coming just a bit too fast,
A little breathless, despite the ease of manner,
An athlete drawing near the tape's last gasp
Yet trying hard to seem still vigorous there.
But no, this metaphor has too much muscle;
His was an indoor art and every phrase
Was handled with a trained seducer's care.
I took the words to heart, or, if not heart,
Some region underneath intelligence,
The area where the hot romantic aria
And certain kinds of poetry are received.
And this Giovanni of the fast buck knew
My humming brain was pleasurably numb;
My limbs were weakening; he would soon achieve
The now sequestered ends for which he'd come.

At last I nodded, glazed, and said I'd sign,
But he showed little proper satisfaction.
He sighed and sounded almost disappointed,
And I remembered hearing someone say
No Juan really likes an easy lay.
But I'll say this: he covered up quite quickly
And seemed almost as ardent as before
When he pressed my hand and said that he was happy
And hoped that I was, too.
                              And then the door
Was closed behind him as our deal was closed.
If something happened I was covered now.
Odd that I felt so chilly, so exposed.

A Note for Biographers

Those early chapters are the ones to watch:
It is too cosily assumed that all
That happens to the eminent will clutch
The reader's buttonhole. Where infants crawl
Is much the same for every baby born,
And later, when the subject walks erect
In private park or back street of a town
The difference is much less than you'd expect.
The little master in expensive tweed
And scabby little mister in huge cap
Suck in same air, are laughed at, bored, afraid:
Their joys and terrors more than overlap,
They are identical. When Christopher
Crouched by father's side to sight that deer
The nightmare that he'd long been tensing for
Banged loud, awake, and father saw his fear.
The boy felt terrible, but no more so
Than little Eddie when Mum said she knew
About the Sunday penny meant to go
Dark in the soft religious bag, not to
The shop which sold sweet paper bags of guilt.
When Christopher was given his Hornby Train
His joy was bright as rails; but Eddie felt
As much delight to wear Dad's watch and chain
Although the watch's pulse had given up
And neither fly-blue arm would move again.
All children's lives are very much alike,
So my advice is keep that early stuff
Down to a page or two. Don't try to make
Nostalgia pay: we've all had quite enough.
What captivates and sells, and always will,

Is what we are: vain, snarled up, and sleazy.
No one is really interesting until
To love him has become no longer easy.

Moral Problem

Impartial dark conceals the true relation
And hides his screwed grimace, the eyeless grin;
His wife receives his violent visitation,
With muffled cries of welcome lets him in.
His vehement dream reshapes her body to
The sweet task that he really wants to do.

His brother exiled to a foreign city,
Months from his heart's address, his candid bed,
Writes to his love a letter long and witty
But leaves frustration's vocables unsaid;
But lust and longing urge him like a knife
To buy a whore and dream he's with his wife.

And who commits adultery? I question:
The one whose need invokes the girl next door
And makes his wife a page in his hot fiction,
Or he who loves his wife inside a whore?
The question whimpers, asking to be fed;
Better all round to wring its neck instead.

When We Were Married

She took the book from the shelf
And turned the pages slowly.
'I loved this book,' she said,
'When we were married.

'That song that teases silence
Was a favourite of mine;
It did not grow tedious
While we were married.

'I ate some food tonight
But did not relish it.
It was a dish that I enjoyed
When we were married.

'When we were married,' she said,
And her lashes were glistening,
'I felt at home in this house, that bed.'
But the man was not listening.

Taken in Adultery

Shadowed by shades and spied upon by glass
Their search for privacy conducts them here,
With an irony that neither notices,
To a public house; the wrong time of the year
For outdoor games; where, over gin and tonic,
Best bitter and potato crisps, they talk
Without much zest, almost laconic,
Flipping an occasional remark.
Would you guess that they were lovers, this dull pair?
The answer, I suppose, is yes, you would.
Despite her spectacles and faded hair
And his worn look of being someone's Dad
You know that they are having an affair
And neither finds it doing them much good.
Presumably, in one another's eyes,
They must look different from what we see,
Desirable in some way, otherwise
They'd hardly choose to come here, furtively,
And mutter their bleak needs above the mess
Of fag-ends, crumpled cellophane and crumbs,
Their love-feast's litter. Though they might profess
To find great joy together, all that comes
Across to us is tiredness, melancholy.
When they are silent each seems listening;
There must be many voices in the air:
Reproaches, accusations, suffering
That no amount of passion keeps elsewhere.
Imperatives that brought them to this room,
Stiff from the car's back seat, lose urgency;
They start to wonder who's betraying whom,
How it will end, and how did it begin—

The woman taken in adultery
And the man who feels he, too, was taken in.

The Old Books

They were beautiful, the old books, beautiful I tell you.
You've no idea, you young ones with all those machines;
There's no point in telling you; you wouldn't understand.
You wouldn't know what the word beautiful means.
I remember Mr Archibald—the old man, not his son—
He said to me right out: 'You've got a beautiful hand,
Your books are a pleasure to look at, real works of art.'
You youngsters with your ball-points wouldn't understand.
You should have seen them, my day book, and sales ledger:
The unused lines were always cancelled in red ink.
You wouldn't find better kept books in the City;
But it's no good talking: I know what you all think:
'He's old. He's had it. He's living in the past,
The poor old sod.' Well, I don't want your pity.
My forty-seventh Christmas with the firm. Too much to drink.
You're staring at me, pitying. I can tell by your looks.
You'll never know what it was like, what you've missed.
You'll never know. My God, they were beautiful, the old
    books.

Tightrope Walker

High on the thrilling strand he dances
Laved in white light. The smudged chalk faces
Blur below. His movements scorn
And fluently insult the law
That lumps us, munching, on our seats,
Avoiding the question that slyly tweaks:
How much do we want to see him fall?
It's no use saying we don't at all.
We all know that we hate his breed.
Prancing the nimble thread he's freed
From what we are and gravity.
And yet we know quite well that he
Started just as we began,
That he, like us, is just a man.
(We don't fall off our seats until
We've drunk too much or are feeling ill.)
But he has trained the common skill,
Trained and practised; now tonight
It flogs our credence as high and white
In the spotlight's talcum he pirouettes,
Lonely, scorning safety nets,
The highly extraordinary man.
But soon, quite softly, boredom starts
Its muffled drilling at our hearts;
A frisson of coughs and shuffles moves
Over the crowd like a wind through leaves.
Our eyes slide down the air and walk
Idly round the tent as talk
Hums on denial's monotone.
It's just as well the act ends soon
Or we would leave, though not stampede,

Leave furtively in twos and threes,
Absence flooding the canvas house
Where he, alone, all unaware
Would go on dancing on the almost air
Till fatigue or error dragged him down,
An ordinary man on ordinary ground.

Peerless Jim Driscoll

I saw Jim Driscoll fight in nineteen ten.
That takes you back a bit. You don't see men
Like Driscoll any more. The breed's died out.
There's no one fit to lace his boots about.
All right son. Have your laugh. You know it all.
You think these mugs today that cuff and maul
Their way through ten or fifteen threes can fight:
They hardly know their left hand from their right.
But Jim, he knew: he never slapped or swung,
His left hand flickered like a cobra's tongue
And when he followed with the old one-two
Black lightning of those fists would dazzle you.
By Jesus he could hit. I've never seen
A sweeter puncher: every blow as clean
As silver. *Peerless Jim* the papers named him,
And yet he never swaggered, never bragged.
I saw him once when he got properly tagged—
A sucker punch from nowhere on the chin—
And he was hurt; but all he did was grin
And nod as if to say, 'I asked for that.'
No one was ever more worth looking at;
Up there beneath the ache of arc-lamps he
Was just like what we'd love our sons to be
Or like those gods you've heard about at school . . .
Well, yes, I'm old; and maybe I'm a fool.
I only saw him once outside the ring
And I admit I found it disappointing.
He looked just—I don't know—just ordinary,
And smaller, too, than what I thought he'd be:
An ordinary man in fact, like you or me.

Time for a Quick One

Noon holds the city back;
Its suburbs are five miles away
Where the baker's cry is greyer than the sky
And drapes itself about the television masts.

Here, alcohol explodes
In secret salvoes, glasses chime.
The stew of noise boils over, spills outside,
Calls hungry volunteers to join the garrison.

A veteran lights a fag.
His face is pigmented with rage,
Flayed raw by booze; both eyes have gone to bed.
A new recruit salutes and takes his life in hand.

Malingerers and old sweats,
Stout corporals and cute subalterns
Shout for reinforcements and more rations.
The smoke cuts harsh at eyes and din thumps louder drums.

Outside, the suburbs start
Their noiseless, disciplined advance.
The city waits with finger firm on trigger.
The fort is now surrounded. Soon closing-time will strike.

Ruminant

The leather belly shades the buttercups.
Her horns are the yellow of old piano keys.
Hopelessly the tail flicks at the humming heat;
Flies crawl to the pools of her eyes.
She slowly turns her head and watches me
As I approach; her gaze is a silent moo.
I stop and we swap stares. I smoke. She chews.

How do I view her then? As pastoral furniture,
Solid in the green and fluid summer?
A brooding factory of milk and sausages,
Or something to be chopped to bits and sold
In wounded paper parcels? No, as none of these.
My view is otherwise and infantile,
But it survives my own sour sneers.
It is the anthropomorphic fallacy
Which puts brown speculation in those eyes.
But I am taken in: that gentleness endears,
As do the massive patience and submission
Huge among buttercups and flies.
But, in the end, it is those plushy eyes,
The slow and meditative jaws, that hold
Me to this most untenable of views:
Almost, it seems, she might be contemplating
Composing a long poem about Ted Hughes.

My Pen Has Ink Enough

My pen has ink enough; I'm going to start
A piece of verse, but suddenly my heart
And something in my head jerks in reverse.

I can't go on—I did, with switch in tense,
And here's the bleak, accusing evidence;
I don't know why, or even what I seek.

This thought jabbed hard: how insolent to make
These blurred attempts when Shakespeare, Donne and Blake
Have done what they have done. And yet it tempts,

This longing to make wicks of words, light lamps
However frail and dim. And, hell, why not?
I've had six children yet more casually got.

Epithets of War—I: August 1914

The bronze sun blew a long and shimmering call
Over the waves of Brighton and Southend,
Over slapped and patted pyramids of sand,
Paper Union Jacks and cockle stalls;
A pierrot aimed his banjo at the gulls;
Small spades dug trenches to let the channel in
As nimble donkeys followed their huge heads
And charged. In the navy sky the loud white birds
Lolled on no wind, then, swinging breathless, skimmed
The somersaulting waves; a military band
Thumped and brayed, brass pump of sentiment;
And far from the beach, inland, lace curtains stirred,
A girl played Chopin while her sister pored
Over her careful sewing; faint green scent
Of grass was sharpened by a gleam of mint,
And, farther off, in London, horses pulled
Their rumbling drays and vans along the Strand
Or trundled down High Holborn and beyond
The Stadium Club, where, in the wounded world
Of five years later, Georges Carpentier felled
Bulldog Joe Beckett in a single round.
And all is history; its pages smell
Faintly of camphor and dead pimpernel
Coffined in leaves, and something of the sand
And salt of holiday. But dead. The end
Of something never to be lived again.

Epithets of War—III: Casualties

They were printed daily in the newspapers.
A woman in Nottingham went mad reading them;
She drowned herself in the Trent.
Her name was not included in the casualty lists.

She was mother of two million sons.
At night a frail voice would quaver,
Cry from its bed of mud:
'Stretcher-bearers! Stretcher-bearers!' She could not go.

She could not bear it. Her mind broke.
Barbed-wire scrawled illiterate history
Over the black dough of Belgian fields,
Was punctuated by anatomies.

In Trafalgar Square an English lady
Distributed white feathers among civilians.
Children with sad moustaches and puttee'd calves
Prepared to be translated.

The crazed mother heard them at night
Crying as hot stars exploded
And the earth's belly shook and rumbled
With giant eructations.

The ambulances lurched through the mire in the brain;
Uniformed surgeons in crimson aprons
Laboured at irreparable bodies;
Dawn bristled on their skullish jaws.

And two million of an innocent generation,
Orphaned by a doomed, demented mother,
Unlearned an axiom: they discovered
Only the lucky few meet death once only.

Epithets of War—V: Eidolon Parade

A grey wind prowls across the lake of stone,
The flag flicks like a summer horse's tail,
The brass voice of the bugle climbs and clings
High before it crumbles, falls and fades.
C.S.M. Hardy, back from Salerno Beach,
Glitters with sea salt, winkles nest in his eyes,
But his voice grinds loud as ever as he calls
The Nominal Roll: Corporal Mick McGuire
Has returned from Alamein, each orifice
Is clogged with sand; but tonight he will appear
Once more at the Church Hall, battle-dress pressed
And patent leather highlights on his feet;
And when the lights are dimmed, the last waltz makes
Its passionate interrogation: *Who's
Taking You Home Tonight?* who but McGuire,
Although his terrible kiss will taste of sand
Gritting on shocked teeth, and his cold cheek
Will seem to her a stony reprimand.
And, while the Corporal tangoes, Private Bain,
A bunch of quarrels hanging from each wrist,
Will sluice his guts with twenty black-and-tans;
But he stands still now, sober, at attention
With that small company paraded there
Waiting for inspection: Dodger Rae,
Equipment scruffy and an idle bootlace,
Is put on an eternal two-five-two;
Spike Liston, gaunt as a Belsen boy or saint
Still rages for more grub; Bull Evans broods
On all the thighs he'll never lie between
Or lie about, his pack and pouches stuffed
With fantasies and condoms; Les King, who crooned

76

Like Bing, is back from Mareth where he lay,
The tunes mislaid, gargling with his blood.
His songs are out of date. And there are others
Whose faces, though familiar, fade and blur.
The bugle publishes another cry.
Two more commands explode; butts and boots
Crash and ring; another echoing shout
And, by the left, they start to march away.
The steady tramping dims into a mist.
The stone ground stretches in its vacancy;
One final flick of flag, the mist comes down,
And silence stuns with its enormous weight,
And there is nothing left to do but sleep.

View from a Wheelchair

Every day is visiting day;
There are no temporal restrictions.
You cannot tell them to go away;
They fuss, or are negligent, or bored.
The world is an open ward
Populated by nurses, orderlies,
And simpering visitors with flowers.
I resent with equal rancour
Both indifference and pity.
Children insult me with their agility.
I am an old baby with a blue chin,
At night my teeth snarl in a tumbler.
As evening darkens in my ward
There are voices from beyond,
Clear cries of the unmutilated,
Murmur of sensual conspiracy,
Salutations, prodigal laughter:
The blind effrontery of health.
I will strangle my ears; I will call
And demand to be put to bed.
But I do not pray for a miracle—
You must not deceive yourself there—
And you must not assume my condition
Is not of my own choosing. I am not sure.
I am less unfortunate, maybe,
Than your insolent pity believes:
The muscles in my wheels do not get tired;
Like a horse I can sleep standing.
And there is something sacred about me,
Something that can haunt, and make you tremble.
I am sick of the fear, the pity, the revulsion.

I want them to put me to bed.
Their gratitude for my not being them
Is a nauseous, poisonous toffee.
It is dark and cold. They must put me to bed.
They do not know that I walk in my sleep.

Uncle Edward's Affliction

Uncle Edward was colour-blind;
We grew accustomed to the fact.
When he asked someone to hand him
The green book from the window-seat
And we observed its bright red cover
Either apathy or tact
Stifled comment. We passed it over.
Much later, I began to wonder
What curious world he wandered in,
Down streets where pea-green pillar-boxes
Grinned at a fire-engine as green;
How Uncle Edward's sky at dawn
And sunset flooded marshy green.
Did he ken John Peel with his coat so green
And Robin Hood in Lincoln red?
On country walks avoid being stung
By nettles hot as a witch's tongue?
What meals he savoured with his eyes:
Green strawberries and fresh red peas,
Green beef and greener burgundy.
All unscientific, so it seems:
His world was not at all like that,
So those who claim to know have said.
Yet, I believe, in war-smashed France
He must have crawled from neutral mud
To lie in pastures dark and red
And seen, appalled, on every blade
The rain of innocent green blood.

Cigarette

It tap-danced on the shining silver case,
Jumped to his mouth, wagged jaunty from teasing lip,
Its whiteness darkening the uncle face;
Thin snake's blue ghost rose curling from the tip.
Emblem of manhood and emancipation,
But something more: it burned yet was renewed
Pure as before; scent stirred sweet perturbation
In the thrilled blood, first inkling of the feud,
Still unresolved, between desire and fear.
My first cigarette was smoked in the boiler shed
Behind the Sunday School in my tenth year.
Veil-dance of smoke revolved in my dazed head,
Strong the sense of falling, though I stood;
I thought that I did wrong, and think so still.
They told us that tobacco-smoking would
Stunt our growth. They tell us now fags kill,
And I believe, though when I ruminate
I see that even smokeless inhalations
Are paces, if not quite so long and straight,
Towards the darkest of all destinations.
I take another, light it, noting how
The stained air holds no sweet reverberations
And that I have no sense of falling now.

View from a Barber's Chair

In the glacial mirror
The skull is preserved;
Dun flesh clings to it
Obstinately alive.
The basin below
Is smooth and white—
Hard flesh of shelled egg—
Taps gleam like spoons.
The head is perched
On a white mound,
Its eyes aggrieved.
Behind, in the gloom,
White deference bends,
Snips and combs;
A glimmer of scissors
Kisses, bites,
Snips locks that, falling,
Tickle the air,
Fall faster than leaves
But quiet and light
On the slope of snow.
Electric buzz
And nibble at neck;
Sweet buzz replies
Warm in the blood;
Surrender's signal,
A yielding hum,
Purred submission
Invite violation,
A numb need
For a cruel Todd,

Which dies away
When the bowing voice
Tickles the ear:
'Next gentleman, please.'
The white mound melts,
Slides down the glass
And disappears.
The stunned head hangs
Amazed a moment,
Then floats away.
The mirror gurgles
In the basin's throat.
The next gentleman
Is gowned in snow.

A Song to Celebrate

Your hair tastes of darkness.
The sea fondles the long drowned.
The shore extends a delicate limb,
The waves relish its whiteness.

Your mouth tastes of moonlight.
The city revs its dark engines;
Lamps are bright burs on the night's coat.
I would wear you like a cloak

And would be your robe for all weathers.
Your flesh tastes of sunlight.
The sea concedes defeat. The drowned
Rise white and dance naked.

The Rivals

All, all of them wanted her.
I watched them, ready to frustrate
Whatever strategy they used,
Doubly armed with fear and hate:
Prince Mincing and Lord Bulge were there,
Paul Profile and Lance Glitterteeth,
Sir Timothy Tarmac, hand on hilt
And golden blade half out of sheath.
I blocked her view when they came flaunting
Their wealth, fine clothes, virility,
Firm jaw, white smile of dancing master;
I showed my own agility.
But there was one whose gaunt appeal
I had not reckoned with. She fell
For him, the one I'd overlooked,
She, with her dainty sense of smell,
Fastidious ways, she fell for him,
The bony one with stinking breath
And sergeant's stripes, the clever fellow
In whose small room she lies beneath
A stiff cold quilt, without a pillow.

The Moth

'The moth has got into it.'
I heard the woman speak from another room.
What the moth had entered I did not know,
Nor why that singular creature should own
The definite article before its name.
The woman said 'The moth' as she might say
'The dog', a minor member of the family,
Yet in my mind's commodious bestiary
There was no space for such a stray.
I knew that it was time for me to go.
I crept away. I left some clothes:
A sweater, vest, two pairs of socks with holes.
Sometimes I think of the moth in its cage,
Its great khaki wings heavy with dust
And the woman feeding it, pushing through the bars
The tasteless garments to assuage
An appetite that must
Make do with such rough food as she, too, must.

Wife Killer

He killed his wife at night.
He had tried once or twice in the daylight
But she refused to die.

In darkness the deed was done,
Not crudely with a hammer-hard gun
Or strangler's black kid gloves on.

She just ceased being alive,
Not there to interfere or connive,
Linger, leave or arrive.

It seemed almost as though
Her death was quite normal and no
Clue to his part would show.

So then, with impunity,
He called up that buttocky beauty
He had so long longed to see

All covering gone: the double
Joggle of warm weighty bubbles
Was sweet delirious trouble.

And all night, all night he enjoyed her;
Such sport in her smooth dimpled water;
Then daylight came like a warder.

And he rose and went down to the larder
Where the mouse-trap again had caught a
Piece of stale gorgonzola.

His wife wore her large woollen feet.
She said that he was late
And asked what he wanted to eat,

But said nothing about the murder—
And who, after all, could have told her?
He said that he fancied a kipper.

A Simple Need

Well, no. Not now I suppose. Not now.
Not in the eyes of the law, I'm not any longer
Married. Yet still I feel she belongs to me,
In a way. Not that she ever really did,
Belong to me I mean. Right from the start I felt
That she was marking time, rehearsing, using me
As stand-in for the genuine first night.
Well, time will mark her in its own good time,
Though that's not what I want. I'm not vindictive.
I'd hate to see her sucked dry by the years.
She always seemed so ripe. I used to think
She's like a plum, a big plum with the smooth
Bloom on summer skin, a plum of plums,
The way they halve! Ridiculous, I know.
But listen, let me tell you something. Listen.
I never caught her out. I never once.
I'd come back two days early from a trip,
Wait till the lights were out. I'd leave the car
A block away and creep up pussyfoot.
I never caught them at it. Never once.
The joke is she got rid of me. Cruelty she said.
I can't go near. Not now. They'd jail me if I did.
But one of these fine nights I'll go,
I've got to go. Just to see them at it once,
That's all. Just see the two of them.
It's only fair.
Drink up. We've time for just one more.
That's all I want: Just see them at it once.

The Mourners

The boy was dead, his body lay
In the smart box.
The vicar said that death and life
Compose a paradox.

Maybe. I watched the father, who
Had not seen
His son for eighteen months or more,
Face raised like a tragic queen;

Tears candidly confessed his grief,
Marched from his eyelids,
Medalled his cheeks. Some time now since
He left his wife and kids.

No histrionics from the wife,
No jewellery of tears;
She would leave for home, a cold house,
Light lamps against her fears,

Build fires against the evening chill,
And yet not cry;
Feed the living children; pray
That none of these would die.